I Wonder Why
I Blink
and other questions about my body
Brigid Avison

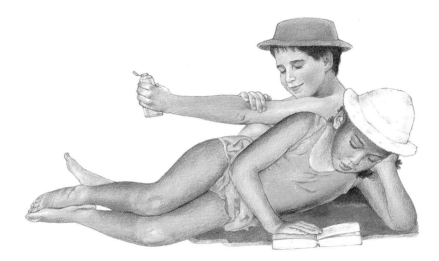

KINGFISHER
BOSTON

KINGFISHER
a Houghton Mifflin Company imprint
222 Berkeley Street
Boston, Massachusetts 02116
www.houghtonmifflinbooks.com

First published in hardcover in 1993
First published in paperback in 1997
First published in this format in 2003

10 9 8 7 6 5 4 3

IMAG/0606/SHA/RNB/126.6MA

LIBRARY OF CONGRESS CATALOGING-IN-PUBLICATION DATA
Avison, Brigid.
    I wonder why I blink and other questions about my
body/Brigid Avison:—1st American ed.
        p.   cm.
    Includes index.
    Summary: In a question and answer format
addresses basic physiology such as why one has
bones, why one needs food, and how the body grows.
    1. Human anatomy—Juvenile literature.
[1. Body, Human. 2. Human physiology. 3. Questions
and answers.] I Title.
QM27.A93 1993
612—dc20 92-45599 CIP AC

ISBN 0-7534-5610-9
ISBN 978-07534-5610-1

Printed in Taiwan

Series editor: Jackie Gaff
Serie designer: David West Children's Books
Consultants: Dr. Elizabeth D. A. McCall Smith,
    Dr. Peter Rowan
Art editor: Christina Fraser
Cover illustrations: Ruby Green, cartoons by Tony
    Kenyon (B. L. Kearley Ltd.)
Illustrations: Chris Forsey 4, 5, 6, 7, 8–9, 10–11,
    12–13, 16–17, 18–19, 20–21; Ruby Green (figure
    illustrations) 5, 6–7, 10–11, 25, 26–27, 28–29,
    30–31; Tony Kenyon (B. L. Kearley) all cartoons;
    Linda Worrall (Linden Artists) 14–15, 18, 22–23

CONTENTS

Is my body the same as everyone else's?

● Every person's body has all the important parts shown below.

You are the only person exactly like you in the whole world — that makes you very special!

But although you are different from everyone else, your body is made of the same things as theirs. And it has exactly the same parts doing all the different jobs that keep you alive.

Brain

Nose

Mouth

Nerves

Blood vessels

Lungs

Muscles

Bones

Liver

Heart

Stomach

4

● These are some of the parts of the body that can be different.

Hair can be dark, fair, or red, curly, wavy, or straight.

Eyes can be different shades of blue, brown, gray, or green.

Noses are different shapes.

Some people have freckles.

Muscles can be big or small.

Skin comes in lots of different colors.

Some people are tall, some are small.

Some people are fat, some are thin.

● Can you see the wavy lines in the skin on your fingertips? They are your fingerprints. No one else in the whole world has the same fingerprints as you.

What is inside my head?

The most exciting and important part of your body is hidden inside your head, beneath your hair, your skin, and your hard skull bone. It is your brain.

Your brain is the part of you that thinks and remembers. It also makes sure the rest of your body is doing what it should!

● Your brain has two sides. The right side of your brain takes care of the left side of your body, while the left side takes care of the right side of your body.

● People's brains come in different sizes. But bigger brains don't make people smarter — any more than having big feet makes them better runners!

- Nerves tell your body what's happening to it — like whether water feels too hot or too cold.

- Messages travel very fast along your nerves. The quickest go as fast as 250 miles an hour (400 km/h)!

- Your nerves start in your brain, then travel in a thick bundle down your back (inside your backbone). From there they branch out to every part of your body.

What makes me feel things?

Every minute of the day your brain is being sent messages about all the different things that are happening inside and outside your body. Some are about things you feel. All the messages travel to your brain along paths called nerves.

- Hurt or pain are feelings that tell you if something is wrong. They are your body's warning system. It hurts when you stub your toe because your body is telling you to stop — something is in your way!

How many bones do I have?

When you were born, you had more than 300 bones. But by the time you finish growing, you will have just over 200!

The missing bones won't have fallen out or disappeared. Instead, as you get older, some of your smaller bones will join together to make bigger ones.

● Without bones inside you to give you a shape, you'd be like a floppy, squishy bag.

Thighbone

● The longest bone in your body is the one above your knee, called your thighbone.

● Your bones are partly made of hard stony stuff called calcium, but unlike stones they are alive. They get bigger as you grow up.

Foot bones

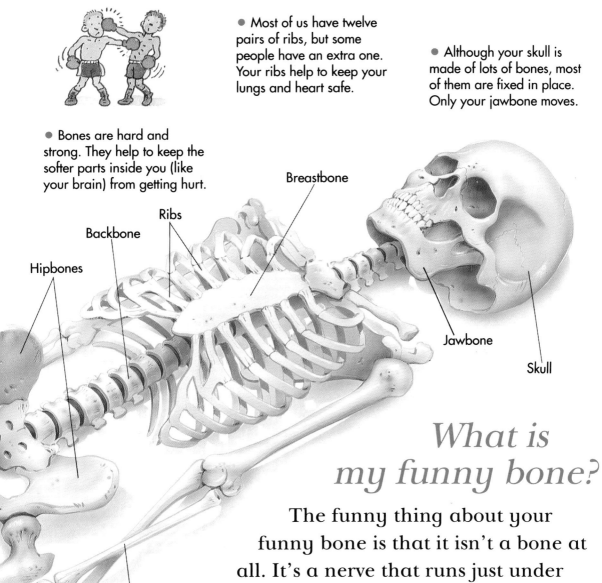

• Most of us have twelve pairs of ribs, but some people have an extra one. Your ribs help to keep your lungs and heart safe.

• Although your skull is made of lots of bones, most of them are fixed in place. Only your jawbone moves.

• Bones are hard and strong. They help to keep the softer parts inside you (like your brain) from getting hurt.

Breastbone

Ribs

Backbone

Hipbones

Jawbone

Skull

Arm bones

Hand bones

What is my funny bone?

The funny thing about your funny bone is that it isn't a bone at all. It's a nerve that runs just under your skin over each elbow. If you bang your elbow, the nerve is banged, too. It sends a message to your brain and you feel pain!

What is my skin for?

Skin is the stretchy bag you live in. It covers your whole body, holding your insides in and protecting them from the outside world.

● Your skin gets its color from something called melanin. People with dark skin have more melanin than people with light skin.

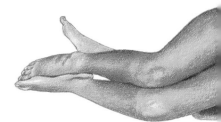

How thick is my skin?

In most places, your skin isn't much thicker than cardboard. But although it is so thin, lots of things happen inside it. Hair grows in skin, and sweat is made there. Skin also has blood vessels, and nerves to send messages to your brain.

Hair grows out of a pit called a follicle.

Nerve-ending

Hair muscle

Blood vessels

What are goose bumps?

When a cat is cold, its fur fluffs up. This traps a blanket of air next to its skin to keep it warm. Your hair also stands up when you are cold and shivery, and goose bumps are made by tiny hair muscles tightening. This doesn't keep you very warm, though, because you aren't hairy enough!

● Whether your skin is light or dark, too much sun can burn you. Wear a hat and put on a layer of sun protection cream.

● Sweat is salty water that your body makes when it's hot, to help keep you cool.

Sweat comes out of holes called pores.

Sweat-making gland

How do I move?

Muscles make you move, by pulling your bones around. When you smile or cry, speak or eat, walk or skip, muscles are doing the work.

- A muscle can only make itself shorter. It needs another muscle pulling the other way to stretch it out again.

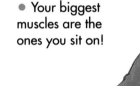

- Your biggest muscles are the ones you sit on!

Why do strong people have big muscles?

- Many tennis players have bigger muscles in the arm they use to hold their racket.

Muscles get bigger and stronger if they are used a lot. That's why athletes practice hard and do lots of exercises.

• To make a bone move, a muscle gets shorter. This pulls the bone one way. To pull the bone back again, another muscle gets shorter. Muscles are attached to your bones by strong white strings called tendons.

Tendon —

This muscle tightens to bend your arm.

When this muscle tightens, your arm straightens.

What is a cramp?

A cramp is when a muscle suddenly feels tight and painful. It stops moving properly and it feels as if it's stuck. No one is quite sure why a cramp happens, but it goes away if you rest the sore spot. Rubbing it can also help.

• Have you ever had a stitch after running? It's a pain in your side, just under your ribs. It means you have a cramp in the breathing muscle below your lungs.

13

Why do I breathe?

You pull air into your body when you breathe. And air is something your body cannot do without, even for just a few minutes.

This is because air has a gas called oxygen in it, and your body needs oxygen to live and grow.

● When you breathe in, air goes down your windpipe to your lungs. These are like big sponges that hold air instead of water.

● If you fold your arms across your chest and breathe in, you'll feel your lungs getting bigger as they fill up with air.

Windpipe

Lungs

Why do I get hiccups?

There's a big muscle below your lungs which helps you to breathe. It's called your diaphragm. You hiccup when something makes this muscle pull down really hard, drawing lots of air into your lungs. To keep too much air from rushing in, a flap at the top of your windpipe clamps down. This closes off the air flow so quickly that your whole body jerks.

● "HIC" is air rushing in.

● "CUP" is the flap clamping down over your windpipe.

What makes me sneeze?

If dust or germs get into your nose, your body makes you sneeze to get rid of them. Your lungs shoot air out, clearing your nose.

● When you sneeze, air rushes down your nose at over 100 miles an hour (160 km/h)!

What does my heart do?

Your heart is a very special muscle which keeps blood moving around your body.

If you put your hand on your chest near your heart, you'll feel it beating. Each time it beats, it pumps blood out around your body.

- To hear a heart beating, find somewhere quiet and rest your ear against a friend's chest. You should hear two sounds close together—"lub-dub, lub-dub."

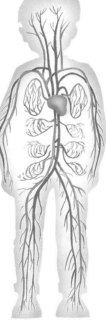

- Blood travels around your body in thin tubes called blood vessels.

- Your body is using up oxygen all the time, keeping you alive, so it has to keep getting more from your lungs.

Blood from your head

To the body

Blood from your body

- One side of your heart pumps blood to your lungs to get oxygen. The other side pumps it around your body.

Blood to your lungs

Blood from your lungs

Blood with oxygen

Blood without oxygen

What is blood for?

- Some insects have blue or green blood.

Your blood is like a fast-moving river flowing around your body. It carries useful things — like oxygen from the air you breathe, and the goodness from the food you eat — to every part of you. It also helps your body to fight germs.

- When you were a baby, you had less than a quart (a liter) of blood — not quite enough to fill a milk carton. When you grow up, you will have about 5 quarts (5 liters) of blood — enough to half fill a bucket!

How big is my heart?

Our hearts grow with us — they get bigger as we do. Whatever size you are now, your heart will be a bit bigger than your fist.

Why do I blink?

Your eyes make tears all the time, not only when you cry. Blinking spreads the tears across your eyes and stops them from drying out and getting sore.

● The iris is the colored part of your eye. It works a little like curtains on a window — when it's too dark to see, the iris opens to let in more light. When the light is too bright, the iris tightens up to protect the eye.

● A blink lasts for about one-third of a second. You do it thousands of times a day.

● Eyelashes help to keep things like dust and grit from getting into your eyes.

Eyelash

Pupil

Iris

● The black hole in the middle of the eye is called the pupil.

• Jellylike stuff in your eyeball keeps it in shape, like air in a balloon.

Why can't I see in the dark?

You can't see much when it's dark, because eyes need light to see. If you look at your eyes in a mirror, you'll see a black hole in the middle of them. Light bounces off everything around you and in through this hole. Messages are then sent from your eyes to your brain, telling you what you are looking at.

• The lining at the back of the eye is called the retina. The picture that forms here is upside down! Your brain turns it the right way up.

A nerve inside here carries messages to your brain.

• There's a lens at the front of the eye. It makes sure the things you see aren't fuzzy, by making light shine in the right place at the back of the eye.

Why are ears such a funny shape?

The shape of your ears helps them to catch sounds from the air. The sounds then go through your outer ear into the hidden part of your ear, inside your head. Animals like rabbits can move their ears to help them catch sounds.

Why do I feel dizzy when I spin around?

Inside each ear, you have three loop-shaped tubes with watery liquid in them. This swishes around when you spin. Special nerves pick up this movement and tell the brain you are spinning. If you stop suddenly, the liquid goes on swishing around for a little longer. Your brain gets the wrong message and you feel dizzy!

Earlobe

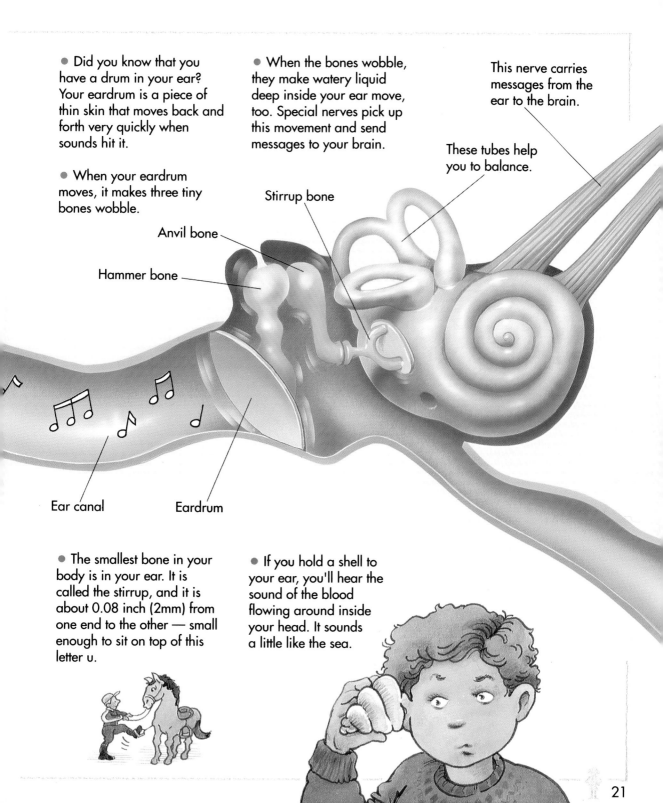

● Did you know that you have a drum in your ear? Your eardrum is a piece of thin skin that moves back and forth very quickly when sounds hit it.

● When your eardrum moves, it makes three tiny bones wobble.

● When the bones wobble, they make watery liquid deep inside your ear move, too. Special nerves pick up this movement and send messages to your brain.

This nerve carries messages from the ear to the brain.

These tubes help you to balance.

Stirrup bone

Anvil bone

Hammer bone

Ear canal

Eardrum

● The smallest bone in your body is in your ear. It is called the stirrup, and it is about 0.08 inch (2mm) from one end to the other — small enough to sit on top of this letter u.

● If you hold a shell to your ear, you'll hear the sound of the blood flowing around inside your head. It sounds a little like the sea.

21

What is my nose for?

Your nose is for smelling things, and it also helps your tongue with tasting. It can do this because tiny bits of food are carried by air up into your nose when you eat.

The bits are much too small to see, but nerves inside your nose find them and send messages about them to your brain.

- When a cold stuffs up your nose, air can't get to the nose nerves and you can't taste your food properly.

- Here's a way to see how much you taste things with your nose. You'll need someone to help you.

1 Get two different flavors of fruit yogurt.

2 Shut your eyes tight and hold your nose.

3 See if you can tell which yogurt you are eating.

- To see how your tongue helps you to speak, put your finger on it and try to say "Hello."

What is my tongue for?

Your tongue is for tasting things, but it also helps you speak and sing. It is covered with tiny little bumps called tastebuds which send messages along nerves to your brain about the food you eat.

Why do teeth fall out?

- When you are grown up, you will have between 28 and 32 teeth.

As you grow up, most parts of your body get bigger. But your teeth can't grow bigger, and so you have to replace them.

When you are small, you have twenty small teeth called milk teeth. These start to fall out when you are five or six years old, to let new, bigger teeth grow in their place.

Where does my food go?

When you swallow food or drink, it gets squeezed down a tube into your stomach. Your stomach squashes and mashes the food into a kind of soup. This "soup" then gets squeezed through a very long winding tube called your intestine. By now, the useful pieces of food are tiny enough to be taken into your blood and carried around your body to give it energy to live and grow.

● Your body tells you it needs food by making you feel hungry.

Why do I go to the bathroom?

There are parts of food that your body can't use. They are pushed along to the end of your intestine. Then, when you go to the bathroom, you push them out through a hole in your bottom called your anus.

● The water your body doesn't need is called urine. This comes out through a different hole.

● It may take a day or two before something you've eaten finishes its journey through your body.

● If air comes back up the tube from your stomach, you make a sound called a burp. Fizzy drinks often make people burp.

Stomach

Appendix   Anus

Intestine

Why does my stomach rumble?

When your stomach has been empty for a few hours, it fills up with airlike stuff called gas. Your stomach may then start the sort of squashing, mashing movements it usually makes when there's food inside it. These squeeze the gas, and it makes a rumbling noise — a little like thunder!

Why do I have to sleep?

Your muscles don't have to do much work when you're asleep, and your brain doesn't have to worry about what's happening in the world around you. Resting these parts of your body gives it a chance to do other jobs. Sleep gives your body time to grow and, if you are ill, to mend itself.

● Babies sleep most of the time because they are growing so quickly.

What is sleepwalking?

Some people get out of bed and walk around while they are still asleep. They don't know they are doing it. When they wake up, they usually can't remember it either!

● Everyone moves when they sleep. You turn over sometimes, or even kick your legs.

- You breathe more slowly when you are asleep, and your heart beats less quickly.

- Many animals dream when they're asleep. Dogs sometimes look as though they're hunting.

What is a dream?

A dream is a story your brain makes up while you sleep. You seem to see and hear things, and it feels as if they are really happening to you.

Sometimes you have happy dreams. Dreams can also be frightening or sad, but they are only happening inside your head.

- A scary dream is called a nightmare. If you get very frightened, you may cry or shout while you are still asleep. The nightmare stops when you wake up.

Why do I get sick sometimes?

When a part of your body stops working properly, you get sick. You don't feel right. Maybe your stomach hurts, or you may have a lot of itchy spots on your skin. Sickness often happens because things called germs get inside your body.

● Sometimes your body has to fight and kill germs. The doctor may give you medicine to help it to do this.

● Some germs like dirt. Washing your body and cleaning your teeth help to keep these germs away.

What are germs?

Germs are tiny living things, far too small to see. There are billions of them on, around, and in you all of the time. Most germs won't hurt you, but some of them can get inside of you—through a cut or if you eat something bad. When this happens, your blood gets to work on the germs and kills them.

Why do I need shots?

The doctor or nurse gives you a shot if a medicine needs to be put straight into your blood. Nobody likes it, but a little scratch or prick is better than being sick for a long time.

● Babies need a lot of shots to help their bodies get ready to fight off germs.

Where do I come from?

You began when a tiny egg inside your mother (no bigger than a period) joined with a tiny bit of your father, called a sperm. Then you grew and grew until you were big enough to be born.

● You stayed in your mother's uterus for about nine months. As you got bigger, her uterus stretched to make space for you.

Uterus

Sperm

Egg

● This is what an egg surrounded by lots of sperm looks like under a microscope.

Uterus

● In the uterus, you floated in a kind of bag filled with water which kept you safe and warm.

● You grew inside your mother in a part of her body called the uterus, or womb.

● When you were ready to be born, the opening of your mother's uterus stretched to let you out.

Umbilical cord — the tube that joined you to your mother.

● As soon as you were born, you took a big gulp of air and started breathing.

● After lots of hard pushing, you popped out of your mother's body through a hole between her legs called her vagina.

What is my belly button?

Your belly button is the place where a special tube joined you to your mother before you were born. The tube had blood vessels in it, so your mother's blood could bring you oxygen and food to keep you alive and growing while you were in her uterus. You didn't need her blood after you were born, so the tube was cut.

Index